P9-AFV-291

Wombats
Stone, Lynn M.

3 2301 00042148 1

DATE DUE		
	MAR 0 1	APR 0 5 2002
NOV 1 6 1993	APR 1 9 1997	
NOV 1 9 1993	MAY 2 7 1997	
FEB 0 5 1994	JUL 1 9 1997	
MAR 2 2 1994	OCT 1 4 1997	
OCT 2 1994	NOV 1 4 1997	
NOV 1 0 1994	FEB 08 1999	
MAR 1 4 1995	MAR 0 4 1999	
AUG 0 9 1995	MAR 1 1 2	
MAP 2 2 1996	MAR 0 7 2001	
JUL 3 0 1996	NOV 2 8 2001	
JAN 2 8 1997	JAN 1 9 2002	

J
599.2
STO

64,911

Stone, Lynn M.
WOMBATS

Community Library
Ketchum, Idaho

WOMBATS

AUSTRALIAN ANIMAL DISCOVERY LIBRARY

Lynn M. Stone

Rourke Corporation, Inc.
Vero Beach, Florida 32964

© 1990 Rourke Corporation, Inc.

All rights reserved. No part of this book
may be reproduced or utilized in any form
or by any means, electronic or mechanical
including photocopying, recording or by any
information storage and retrieval system
without permission in writing from the
publisher.

PHOTO CREDITS

All photos © Lynn M. Stone

ACKNOWLEDGEMENTS

The author thanks the following for photographic assistance:
Lone Pine Koala Sanctuary, Brisbane, Queensland, Australia;
Queensland National Parks and Wildlife Service;
Blue Mountains Tourism Authority, Katoomba, Australia

LIBRARY OF CONGRESS
Library of Congress Cataloging-in-Publication Data
Stone, Lynn M.
  Wombats / by Lynn M. Stone.

    p. cm. — (Australian animal discovery library)
    Summary: An introduction to the shy, nocturnal Australian
wombat.
    ISBN 0-86593-059-7
    1. Wombats—Juvenile literature. [1. Wombats.]
I. Title. II. Series: Stone, Lynn M. Australian animal discovery
library.
QL737.M39S76   1990
599.2—dc20   90-30485
                                 CIP
                                 AC

Wombat

TABLE OF CONTENTS

599.2
570

THE WOMBAT

Everyone in Australia knows the wombat. Well, they know the name wombat, but most Australians have never seen a wild wombat.

The reasons are that wombats are shy and **nocturnal.** Nocturnal animals are active at night. They hide during the day.

Three kinds, or **species,** of wombats live in Australia. They are the northern hairy-nosed wombat *(Lasiorhinus krefftii),* southern hairy-nosed wombat *(Lasiorhinus latifrons),* and common wombat *(Vombatus ursinus).*

Wombats have plump, furry bodies and short legs. They look a bit like bears, or beavers without tails.

Common Wombat

THE WOMBAT'S COUSINS

The wombat belongs to a family of mammals called **marsupials.** Marsupials give birth to very tiny babies which the mother raises in a **pouch.**

The pouch is a pocket of skin and fur under the mother. The best-known pouched animals are kangaroos.

Wombats, as marsupials, are related to kangaroos. Wombats are more closely related, however, to the koala.

Neither wombat nor koala has much of a tail. Both wombat and koala have baby pouches that face backwards.

The wombat's only marsupial relative in North America is the opossum.

Koala

HOW THEY LOOK

Wombats of all species have wide heads, small eyes, and somewhat pointed ears.

Hairy-nosed wombats have softer fur than common wombats. As you would expect, they have hair on their nose, or **muzzle.**

Wombats weigh from about 30 pounds to 75 pounds. They have long, sharp teeth like woodchucks, muskrats, and beavers.

The common wombat can be yellowish, gray, dark brown, or black. Hairy-nosed wombats are dark with patches of white or gray, especially underneath.

Southern Hairy-nosed Wombat

WHERE THEY LIVE

Wombats live only in Australia. The common wombat lives in forests near the sea coast from southeast Queensland to southeast South Australia. It also lives on the island state of Tasmania.

The southern hairy-nosed wombat lives in southeast Western Australia to southeast South Australia. Its home, or **habitat,** is dry woodland or grassland.

The northern hairy-nosed wombat lives only in a small part of east central Queensland.

Wombat habitat: Blue Mountain
National Park, New South Wales

Virginia Opossum

Common Wombat asleep

HOW THEY LIVE

Wombats, like the marmots and badgers of North America, are **burrowers.** They dig holes in the ground with their front feet. They use their back feet to kick soil out of the hole. When a wombat finds a tree root in its way, it bites through it.

Sometimes wombats live in a neighborhood with other wombats. Each wombat, however, has its own burrow.

Wombat burrows can be as long as 90 feet underground.

Wombats are not noisy, but they do hiss and growl.

Southern Hairy-nosed
Wombat by burrow

THE WOMBAT'S BABIES

A mother wombat usually has just one baby. The baby struggles into the mother's pouch immediately after birth.

The baby lives in the pouch for six to seven months. It returns to the pouch to nurse on mother's milk until it is eight or nine months old.

By the age of 10 months, the young wombat leaves its mother's care.

Wombats in captivity have lived as long as 26 years.

Southern Hairy-nosed Wombat

PREDATOR AND PREY

Wombats eat plants. Generally they eat grass, roots, or tree bark. They also eat farm vegetables and sea plants that wash ashore.

The wombat has few enemies except man and dingoes. Dingoes are wild dogs. Like other **predators,** or hunters, they eat other animals, called **prey.**

Baby wombats may also be prey for eagles, owls, foxes, and cats.

Dingo

THE WOMBAT AND PEOPLE

People have been the wombat's enemy for many years. Whole neighborhoods of wombats have been destroyed, usually by farmers.

To farmers, the wombat is a pest. Wombat holes can break the legs of farm animals, and wombats eat farm crops.

Rabbits were brought to Australia from Europe. Rabbits have become a problem because they eat crops. Wombats are sometimes killed when farmers try to poison rabbits. Rabbits hide in wombat burrows.

People have found that captive wombats may become quite tame.

THE WOMBAT'S FUTURE

The number of wombats has dropped. Some of the land where wombats live has been used for farms and buildings. In the future, more land will be used.

Meanwhile, the common wombat still has healthy numbers in many mountain forests. The southern hairy-nosed wombat is not rare either.

The northern hairy-nosed wombat, however, is one of the rarest animals in the world. Only about 60 are left. They are protected in a Queensland national park.

Glossary

burrower (BURR ro er)—an animal which digs a hole (burrow) into the ground

habitat (HAB a tat)—the kind of place an animal lives in, such as a forest

marsupial (mar SOOP ee ul)—a family of mammals in which the females have a pouch for raising the young, which are born not fully formed

muzzle (MUH zull)—the jaws, nose, and mouth of an animal

nocturnal (nohk TUR nal)—active at night

pouch (POWCH)—the mother marsupial's warm pocket of skin in which her baby is raised

predator (PRED a tor)—an animal that kills other animals for food

prey (PREY)—an animal that is hunted by another for food

species (SPEE sheez)—within a group of closely related animals, one certain kind

INDEX